Pigeon Songs

For Katja and Roisín

Pigeons do not sing.
– Kei Miller

Pigeon Songs

Eoghan Walls

Seren is the book imprint of
Poetry Wales Press Ltd.
57 Nolton Street, Bridgend, Wales, CF31 3AE
www.serenbooks.com
facebook.com/SerenBooks
twitter@SerenBooks

The right of Eoghan Walls to be identified as
the author of this work has been asserted in accordance
with the Copyright, Designs and Patents Act, 1988.

ISBN: 978-1-78172-490-3
ebook: 978-1-78172-491-0
Kindle: 978-1-78172-492-7

A CIP record for this title is available from the British Library.

The publisher acknowledges the financial assistance of the Welsh Books Council.

Cover photograph: Jacob Riglin.
www.jacobmedia.com

Author photograph: Paul Maddern.

Printed in Bembo by Latimer Trend & Company Ltd, Plymouth.

Contents

Angry Birds

My father is watching his father die on a lime-green pillow.

The tumours nestle in his crotch like the eggs of a sparrow.

Birds smash into pillars of glass and concrete on my iPhone.

The plastic silhouette of a hawk wards the hospital windows.

Like iron filings, the sky is magnetised with squalls of crows.

I imagine one smashing the glass, splintering its hollow bones.

More. Battering the windowpane to a mesh of feathery holes.

The building jagged with beaks and wings. Corridors tremolo.

Us bearing him out like Tippi Hedren as *The Birds* closes.

Feathers drifting from the vault of the sky like black snow.

The infinite flocks weighing up our claims on a tomorrow.

The Keelhauling of Noah

With Shem's hands bound below deck, out of trouble,
Ham and Shepheth tipped the great man overboard,

knifing the water, to feel each cubit and its barnacles
on the skin of his back. But ever afterwards, he swore

he witnessed such orreries of jellyfish blooming there,
he could map the entire cosmos in their glowing bells.

They multiplied so wild on the nutrients of his people,
he doubted his was the only covenant, as great swarms

loved his face until he blacked out in their tentacles.
He awoke on deck, scalped, with a cursive scripture

of all that lay outside the ark in his looping sores,
and two fingers missing. Borne to the ship's bowels,

warm with dung and the brawling ocelots, he still
found no peace from the faces of his neighbours.

The Universal Blues

This town is a layered skyline of twenty shades of blue,
with blue faces at blue windows under a bright blue moon.

There's a blue girl in a room where the TV spills bad news
across the bare arse of a man who did what he came to do.

Blue is the deoxygenated blood in the lining of her cervix
as white spunk headbutts the future in a frenzy of aquarobics.

It is hard to whisper blues with him spread-eagled on the sofa,
or to reckon your every cell was once the heart of a supernova.

This town is just a bell-curve with us swelling in the middle,
watching our gas-bills and P45s pile up on the coffee table.

But the sperm is a mad sine-wave in the universe of blue,
and the egg is a tight blue nova, and once, the egg was you.

Jubilate Columbidae

I woke this morning with a vibration in my lungs
as if my chest were a dome of murmuring pigeons,
and one cut through the edges of my concentration,
and now my throat swells to her soft clarion.
For she is grey as smoke out of a gun.
For she bothers soldiers around the garrison,
but is too light to carry more than vital information.
For she breeds on any surface she can find a purchase on,
and there is no city she has not found a purchase on.
For she turns half her face to every new commotion,
as her other eye makes sure her getaway is open.
For she startles from the eaves without provocation.
For she flaps like the hymnals of an eager congregation.
For she eavesdrops in the church and the train station.
For her shit is a reminder of all that comes unbidden.
For thus she warns pedestrians to turn their eyes to heaven.
For she kisses out of hunger, which is prudence in affection.
For she eludes starvation.
For she is amicable both free and in captivity.
For she can practise patience in the pockets of magicians.
For she elicits tenderness even from the burliest of men.
For she expresses in the palm the delicacy of engines.
For she does not panic as the traps are sprung.
For she rotates about her axis to find a point on the horizon.
For in her sinuses she bears a mote of magnetic iron.
For this will bring her home.
For she will come home.

The Pigeon on the Egg

the egg is absolute gravitational pull

tho harry sometimes swaps the egg for pebbles
& we who hunger madden waiting on pink muscle

egg the hardest cushion egg the hop eternal
corn the egg rain the egg open sky the egg

tho harry fills our grain with complex butanols
& we whose gonads shrink learn of cramps terrible
wandering mad on tarmac to bite the rumbling axles

egg the winter song egg the kiss cloacal
smoke the egg bone the egg dawn the marbled egg

a sun dies in the yolk when the egg falls
from which we who orbit tug the world impossible

hatching in bordeaux & the cobbled slats of brussels
crowding rooftops forests rafters humming vowels
nothing was before the eaves for we who rustle

tho some don't choose the egg

& breathe keenest lightly flying from kerfuffle
roosting in clear spaces with both horizons visible

eggless those who make life happen with other troubles

Counting Breaths

after Peter Mackay

The heat of the child's quiet puff
fluttering the callus of my thumb.

The heave of the duvet as my wife
warms dark caverns with her bum.

My throat is as dry as a hieroglyph
on this countdown ad infinitum.

Tobacco has left my breath rough
as a dust of glass in my phlegm.

Like Jonah's vespers turning gruff
from sleeping in the whale's gums.

Or anglerfish sucking the cold stuff
near the ocean's clammy bottom.

Kilolitres of the whale's great sniff
skimming briefly from her fathoms.

The wind rebuffed by distant cliffs
backlit in the orange glow of slums.

Refugees' breath on crowded skiffs
watching dark coasts close on them.

A child hefted in a coastguard's lift,
swinging breathless from his arms.

My whole shook breadth as a cough
rocks through my residing phantom.

My wife's caesura, each time I shift
and pause for her to find her rhythm.

The heat of the child's quiet puff
fluttering the callus of my thumb.

My throat is as dry as a hieroglyph
on this countdown ad infinitum.

Pear Stones

Skinning the baby's pear with my teeth,
I dislodge a lump from its grainy flesh,
like a singular gravel beneath the peel,
a warped nut of pear fibres coalesced
from itself, just like tissue may harden
in the ripening of a milk-heavy breast,
but drier – more like the knots of skin
on the cuticles on the hand of a carcass
ossifying in the hermetitude of a coffin –
but as I am footering, the big wet mass
is clawed out of my fingers to her lips,
as she descends on the fruit, ravenous,
first gnawing a pulp from its sugary tip,
working down into the stump and seeds,
the juices and stone, the fibres and pith.

Buoyancy

Rutting bull seals might take pity on me here, caught
mid-coitus in the eyes of my upright child in her cot,

as I'm ballasted from the blues of sub-glacial space,
breathless, towards the holes gnawed in the surface.

My blood decompresses too quickly as I near the air
and a world creaking with the footfall of polar bears.

The stare of the child can barely reflect on anything,
say the seals. Foraging must happen. Turn and sink,

and they're right, but there's more moving in her eyes
than there are shadows treading over the arctic ice.

Ice Bear Dreams

She is a cub again on the long swim south,
treading in the dark wake of her mother
as stars rain, hissing out in the seawater.

Unending rutting. His claws pinch her,
so parched she jaws the powdery drift,
and watches steam plume from her lips.

Her footing slips at the foot of the cliff.
She tumbles skywards past the rank nests
of kittiwakes and the screeching auklets.

Inside each beached whale there is a pit
where the bodies of her long-dead cubs
live peering between the blubbery ribs.

Her paws shrink to a seal's black nubs.
She breathes water and is untouchable.
Bears lumber after her in the blue chill.

Bawling toothlessly she watches her kill
stripped by foxes down to the bare bones,
powerless to raise her paws from the snow.

Horking beached blubber down her throat,
she hears the whale's lungs. Its soft breath
is indistinguishable from her mother's breath.

       The ice is gone. The males have stayed south
       to sweat and brawl on the drylands forever,
       and left her to mewl cubless on the gravel.

The moon burns the blizzard at eyelevel,
until the snow leaves her and the moon alone,
the moonskin warm as a teat against her nose.

The History of Aviation

As Yuang Huangtou was roughhoused off the tower
with a man-sized paper owl strapped to his shoulders,
tumbling face-first into kite-wreckage and prisoners,

when the owl jerked and caught a bellyful of updraft
to bear him in a strong northerly over the Purple Path,
I'd like to think there were a few moments he laughed,

flinging his eyes to the horizon, the way my daughter
empties her red lungs as she casts her arms about her
when I hurl her skywards, a will-it-won't-it laughter,

briefly permitting the thought that falling is optional,
before the lurch comes, tilting the owl back to the soil,
where Gao Yang's men line up at the brow of the hill.

Sunday at the Reliquary

The snakes were gone and Petmania was facing closure,
so we nipped off the high street to pay the church a visit,
stepping from a muggy July for the coolness of St Peter's,

whispering in our T-shirts before the shadowed reliquary,
a black head snarling through the glass, his lips withered,
and my daughter pointed at his teeth and whispered *Scary,*

and I wondered about the brain matter of Oliver Plunkett,
shrivelling like a meaty walnut for the last four centuries,
or did the executioner scoop the skull before he dumped it,

and we lit candles for Fiona and for Granny-in-Heaven,
and the daughter burned her palm and wept a little bit,
as I read a leaflet on the True Cross and the sick women

they used to distinguish duds from the genuine article,
and the dying crone who leaped up like a child of seven,
and it was time to go but the daughter was incorrigible,

soothing her palm in the font, as a flurry of Canadians
bustled in sweaters around the saint in a giddy huddle,
and I swear I saw him blink in the flash of their Canons,

but couldn't risk parking longer with no disabled permit,
so I hoisted the daughter up and shouldered into the sun,
stepping back from the miraculous as we had known it.

The Tooth Burier

Saving crocus bulbs from Otto's grave-earth, she lifted
a quarter-jawbone, with three teeth intact on one ridge.

We had her bury it. But all through the funeral service,
she click-clacked her own loose snaggletooth on her lip.

Two days later we went to see Ötzi in the Ötzi Museum.
Five millennia in the snow had peeled him a pearly grin.

That night I felt her fingers inside my mouth mid-yawn,
to feel the teeth overlapping each other in my lower jaw,

like the Cadmea's lime slabs, lain aslant by the Spartoi,
themselves risen from dragon's teeth pushed in the soil.

This morning, yelps, as the snaggletooth fell in her lap,
a bloody pearl. Her tongue felt out the shock of the gap,

before she ran to stash it in her hairbands. This the third
she has refused to cash, shoring up her hidden seedhoard.

The Principles of Collision

after Kenneth Koch

Once there is collision you can have an event.
Two things bumping is the way change happens.
If a man howls and twists his limbs on the stairs,
we sit watching until his head slams the bannister.
Collision: event. Then we call for an ambulance.
Only when a virus breaches his brain's defences
can it imprint microscopic scars on the synapses.
Two things bump; one surface briefly collapses
into another, and a fallout occurs at the interface.
Consider a narwhal gnashing holes in the sea-ice,
grating its bloodied gums for a mouthful of air,
breaching the sunken world to the threat of bears.
One collision can spawn another. The way a kiss
cascades into another kiss, on and on, relentless,
until all your skin is as raw as a licked battery.
Disagreement is the genesis of each new theory.
Two doctors may collide with a new consultant
before they can agree on the patient's treatment.
It is the central principle of virtual world design.
One icon must meet resistance in another icon
or avatars sink through the surface of the world
to float without direction in an endless universe.
That's how it was before time and space began,
where nothing happened until the first collision.
Two particles touched and everything exploded.
A new book hits the mat; a patient learns to code.
One sperm into one egg. One atom into another.
One stranger in a queue bumps another stranger.
Cascades of incidence when things slam together.
By pressing your skin to the surfaces of weather,
you can leave a room and face the world outside,
permeable at your edges, and ready to collide.

Swimming Lessons

This morning a thump declared a swallow's neck was broken
below the big window. So she demanded a swallow's burial
in the furthest corner of the garden,

and now she hangs like a carcass and watches her fingers bloat
through her goggles, given up on her breathless doggy paddle
for limp drifting, only half-afloat,

gone through the looking glass into pale underworlds of water,
among the light particles and swollen legs, where she struggles
to recall swallow psalms from earlier,

how nests are made by swallows coating their tongues in mud,
how autumn looses typhoons of swallows into oceanic squalls,
but odd fledglings bounce from headbutts

to swing between the earth and air. At the sight of her gutty father
she needs breath, shoulder-blades twisting in their bed of muscles
like twin buried arrowheads of feathers.

Urvertrauen

Dog-bit, the child is distinguished from the leveret
not by the press of frozen peas or a sucked Kit Kat

but the way her howls soften at the plasma screen,
as the fear of death-by-dog and her bloodied knee

fade to enlightenment in the glow of talking pigs,
Coco Pops, or gestation periods of dinosaur eggs,

her breath steadying as ricocheted satellite signals
spill through the cracked heavens in electric jingles,

unlike the bit leveret shuddering under the briars,
as greyhounds rough up the carcass of her mother,

whose only shield is stillness. As her blood dries,
she holds the branching horizons in her wide eyes,

learning her atheism in the thorny greys of the sun,
flat on the mud where she'll feed and fuck and run.

Notes on Repin's *Easter*

Christ stumbles squinting past the rolled tombstone,
one palm low to the hare in benediction. Or hunger.

His eyes are the watery blue of Repin's *Deserter*.
Repin notes of the hare's eyes: *lama sabachthani*.

Contra this, Voloshin: *here comes Christ the clown,*
to breathe new life in her pelt like a balloon animal.

Note the hare's red jowls. She has gorged on the cud
of her flensed shank, and slicked her jaws with foam.

Repin notes: *the hare's breath is grass and blood,*
infused with her own droppings and juniper berries.

Christ's face is crowned with scabs, no visible halo.
The hare's bloodied haunches are tensed to bolt.

Of the one: our dead flesh raised unto song eternal,
slaked on His blood to burrow us free of the earth.

Of the other: canny leverets outstripping the hounds,
their pulses quickened in forms matt with afterbirth.

Her bob is turned. Neither will relinquish the day.
The greys in Christ's beard are the hare's greys.

The Pigeon on Chelmno

o do not carry the breath of life to chelmno
or brush wingtips over the city's grey domes
in feathery haloes through the burnt snow

in the pines after the sonderkommando
empty the last truckload in from kolo

for harry is unpacking dead from the hole

suffering no patience for children & crones
as he lifts one shorn beauty by the elbow
dusting beetles & frozen grit off her bones

& cups her as delicate as a phrenologue

& offers her his lips in a puckered zero
pulling her spine to his chest like a saxophone
unable to hold back a groan in his throat

pealing in the circle of the dead with his o, o, o

The Pale Child

The girl waits as I grope back to bed from a piss,
the faces of our dead superimposed on her face,

whispering softly that the life after us is vicious
but certain. There is a catalogue of our mistakes

that will be replayed in worlds beyond our own,
and all depends on what we have done at home.

Sisyphus in Laytown

On a day so warm the birds speak with human voices
and the mist drags clammily across the beach houses,

a woman is tugging a mattress to the middle landing,
first pulling against the step on which she's standing,

then pushing up from below so it caves around her.
Through the skylight, she hears the seagulls gather

as she hunkers down on a step to catch her breath.
She still has weeks to live, but she carries her death

in her throat, and there is still time for her to give up
and accept that the mattress will never reach the top,

and shut the skylight on the seagulls' joyless banter,
but instead she grasps two fistfuls of mixed polyester

and assaults the climb again, sweat dripping off her,
pushing through failure, each time a little harder.

Kepler-22b

That there was a planet of sea
        on the far edges of the cosmos
                where only heaving tsunamis

disturbed the planet's surfaces,
        that there existed such a world
                where horizons spun endlessly

through an improbable universe
        and nothing ever broke the tide,
                possessed you as student nurses

made a fuss over your PICC line
        those long weeks after Dr Harris
                casually brought up gemcitabine,

as you ate grapes to impress us,
        propped upright on two pillows,
                and I chatted about the abysses,

thinking we shared these shadows,
        the ruins of an alien civilisation,
                great sunk leviathan hollows,

kelp forests shaking with whalesong,
        but lately, I think our imaginations
                were out of synch, and I was wrong,

and that your mind filled with oceans
        where no life could disturb the sea,
                just light adrift in perpetual rotation.

B-Aisling

Shrouds of web fall most thickly over St Stephen's Green.
Bare clothing rails creak in doorways all up Grafton Street.

Higher up, web-cables howl as a dry wind scours the city.
Double-deckers barricade the roads that lead to Trinity.

Rust blooms where vehicles were punctured in their sides.
Cocooned, the statue of Joyce looks like a funeral bride.

Close up, webs are clotted by broadsheets and spent cash.
The buildings creak, bracing in the tension before a crash.

The sky is reflected bleakly in the city's black windows.
Dusk falls unlit. New filaments scoot out from the GPO.

Under bridges, dark limbs clatter the dry bed of the river.
I am back, with a crowbar and a shotgun, for my mother.

This time, the right door bursts in clouds of light and dust.
I cut her fragile bones free from her webbed sarcophagus.

Looking up, we shuffle backwards to the getaway car
and slalom past abandoned lives on the North Circular.

In the mirror, the Hivequeen is tearing up the skyline.
My mother shakes the webs off, surprised to be alive.

Each time, I see her glow more than she ever really did.
Like Jocasta. Celluloid. Butch to my Sundance Kid.

The Pigeon on the Bread Riots

when harry's daughter hits a soldier with a breadroll
a grunt for back-up follows down the radio
& tear-gas flours the airways up al falki road

when harry's daughter holds cloth to her broken nose
she drops breadstuffs & fills her skirt with stones

& we who fly the nile work out when to go
by harry's daughter's choice of what to throw

one day she'll ask harry why he stayed at home
& he'll wax on of gods baking sons in dough

five thousand rioters fed on a couple of fishy loaves

as untaxed grainsacks unload from foreign boats
& cairo's wheat is underdug for export mangoes

as the banks of the nile keep themselves afloat
harry'll draw a line between the body & the soul
& we who mourn grain search rubble for tossed rolls

The Bright and Crayoned Universe

She has drawn them disembarking a sky-blue bus,
fresh from the bombing of Al Hajar. Some stumble
in the red-blobbed orchard, their hair shedding dust.

They are queuing up for their place at the long table.
There's rolls and meat enough for a busload of kids,
a striped jug of milk between two pyramids of apples.

When they are done the table will be cleared for tig.
But one kid stands on his own by the refuse trough
where the mash is mulled over by bright neon pigs.

I ask my daughter why the boy is stood a way off.
She says his shirt's too rough. His outline's wrong.
Says he'll wreck the camp songs with his cough.

No doubt his hammock will be cold in the morning.
He'll head back to the drab streets of Damascus
back in the universe where I have added nothing.

Visitors

Unlacing her halter-top, she said her flesh was silt,
once plush with the pachyderm folds of a newborn,
subsiding yearly from her submerged necropolis,
stretching to a thin velour glaze across her bones.

I sun-creamed her long brown nape and shoulders,
as she leafed the leaflets from the mummy exhibit,
then joined the bare-skinned mobs invading Luxor,
haggling baksheesh and cigarettes with streetkids.

Later on, we exhibited our own bodies in the dark.
Our vellum plucked and pocked, our stretchmarks
like contour maps of cities sunk beneath our skin

that laid bare the shady alleys we would get lost in,
poking through each other's curios and spice-stalls,
puzzling over the glyphs and slogans on the walls.

Moles

Nephews join the dots on his back in the hotel pool,
rolling the weight of the word in their small mouths,

a perfect word, for the fields of him pock with earth,
for the mounds push from within, for their dark hair.

Last spring, he found a mole-cub blinded in our air,
and nudged it alive to the ferns on the tip of his boot,

where a string of moles dried out on the barbed wire
like shucked gloves hung to catch their owner's eyes.

A Slovak girl once spoke of his skin's constellations,
hip-clusters, the trio on his neck, and kissed each one.

These nights he feels them furrowing through his loam,
tugging ribbons of air to the worm-hoard in his bones.

Thornton's Property Services

All Sunday night the windows were left open.
Haar blew through the bathroom and the hall,
obscuring desks and phones and dry-wipe pens
and the photocopier, which had not slept at all.

Findlay tells me he's always the first one in,
and found it humming quietly beneath its lid,
a lone bar of light in the mist, and on a whim,
he hit *Print* just to see what the machine did.

The print-off was warm and soft as belly skin,
and where he had expected a pure blank sheet
were blotches and swirls written upon nothing.

The white oblivion of the page was incomplete,
and he could not look away until the others
crept in through the haar like early raptors.

The Pigeon on the Rollercoaster

dawn at gröna lund & harry is a trespasser

vomit on the asphalt & trees hung with streamers
one sequined jimmy choo toppled in fresh litter
beside a half-drunk bottle of pear cider

after the last taxi & before the streetsweepers
harry walks among the city's abandoned fliers

the closed amusements lined along the river
hopping the fence around the rollercoaster
pulling at the gate marked operatör

& starts to climb the ladder
passing out of stockholm's natural order

mindless of we whose nests his passing bothers
his balance grim & tentative demeanour
tottering breathy now along the girder

where he sits to dangle both legs over
considers the matter he came here to consider
kicking off one shoe & then the other

the air is cool at the surface of the water
colder & breezy as it whistles higher

we who shudder on the girders know the cold as hunger

but whatever happens harry can't see what he came for
so he chooses to return & fetch his footwear
crawling to the ladder a little stiffer

breakfast a question the city always answers

The Weight of Her

Riding my shoulders in the hollows of a ghost estate,
my daughter whispers that she wishes she was dead,

for in the afterlife she will get everything she needs,
such as a tablet that runs forever with dead batteries,

but best of all, her own dead horse, a patchwork nag
of bones and worms to bear her past the zombie dogs,

or if her tights get caught, she'll only have to whistle,
and he'll whinny over to prise her from the brambles.

As we duck under a mantle, the irony's not lost on me,
bearing the chattering weight of little lady Persephone,

and I'd gladly gallop on to suss out the land before her,
but wish she wasn't so easy with this chat. I remember

Mr S. standing for months at the grave of his daughter,
shoulders stooped as if he still bore the weight of her,

his eyeballs as large as a horse's in his skull, transfixed
by the hoofbeats splashing ahead of him down the Styx.

Up the Border

If they come asking, tell them I've gone to walk the border,
where eight-year-olds used to know how to smuggle diesel
past the dragon's teeth, where one field opens onto another,

and a fly-tipped fridge might bristle a ribcage of bluebells,
and you're as like to find schoolkids taking a feed of cider
as a hush of forty-year-olds urging bloodlust from pit-bulls,

where hedges hide porn and barbed wire dangles knickers,
and Nelis swears he once got a girl fresh out of Marseilles
to stretch bareback on the tarmac in the middle of summer,

and the winter the Foyle froze over, submerged to its middle,
he found a fox in the shuck, its entrails and spine uncovered
by jackdaws, ear-tufts and tail-tip blooming out of a puddle

and even though its small face was frozen intact underwater,
he got the sense that if he hacked out and thawed its pupils,
they'd be sharp as lasers with the focus of crossing over.

The Silence of Nudists

I watched an old nudist tonight
wading from the bank of the river,

his frail limbs the glowing white
of a hippo's unsheathed member,

and I had a vision of my death,
transmogrified to a sort of hippo,

the cold water stealing my breath,
sloshing closed across my torso,

until I nosed through silty matter
in the rearing fringes of the murk,

as other hippos treaded the water,
moon-rimmed in the upper dark.

I thought about the loss of gravity
and a hippo's slow tectonic grace,

and how I could dread the clarity
of air on the hollows of my face,

for cold nights always feel colder
as the water dries upon the skin,

and words carried over the water
can sound warped and indistinct.

I do not think that I would float
to listen for our needy daughters

if I could seal my ears and throat
and grub the cold bed of the river,

like a nudist stumbling in a bush
tugging one leg into his trousers

at the first disturbance of the hush
by the snort and rustle of voyeurs.

De Pneuma

You can run until your pulse and moisture and breath
batter their own singular path through the dry nettles

bearing the body like the ice in the heart of a comet
and should it slam into a Citroën, or the heart unhitch

itself from its own vital rhythms in a casual misstep,
the whole meat could be cast like a coat in the ditch

and the pulse and hot breath carry on, startling cattle
and treading leaves at the edge of the football pitch,

the unrefined stuff of the soul according to Aristotle,
at least, if De Pneuma can be attributed to Aristotle.

Peas

Marcus Quintus, best of all Herod's legions,
scavenged peas in Palestine's scrubby borders,
splitting pods to bulk up his piss-poor rations,
mulling his orders.

Raindrops beaded stems in the tangled bushes.
Lightning scalded ozone above the Dead Sea.
Roots remade dead substances in the humus
perfectly as peas,

young and green as Napoli's newest leaf-tips,
best compared to pellets of snow and basil.
Creepers coiled his fingers like baby digits,
awfully gentle.

The Last Connection

The way I came, to get my next connection
meant me hoofing it through central Glasgow
on a night the city was populated by ghosts.
Pale waifs in heels used fliers for protection

from the rain. Blue couples held conversations
in pizza-parlour windows. I stormed the road
head-down, collar-up, trying to light a smoke
and nearly tripped into my mother at the station.

I hugged her, damp; there was so much to ask her
about miscarriages, our troubles buying a home,
the taste of the earth. She listened to me, tender,

but she had someplace to be. I watched her go,
zipping between the buses along Queen Street,
and I caught the nine forty-one for Aberdeen.

Tree Surgeons on the Aberdeen Line

You woke one night to railway tree surgeons
giving the trees by the track their yearly trim
with their hybrid carriage of mechanical limbs.
It was half like Megatron of the Decepticons

and half a visitation of the archangel Metatron,
wailing sawdust with jazzy chainsaw hymns,
whimsically tearing up the trees around him
just as it was all kicking off in your abdomen.

You watched the surgeons in their orange vests
chucking sapling after sapling into the chipper,
and asked me what they did with fallen nests.

I stayed in bed, watching you in your slippers,
with a silhouette so stark against the window
for one brief moment I mistook it for a halo.

When all the Men Turned into Geese

After the emergency brakes and after-throes,
the feathered necks fluting from their collars,
the weepy wife clutching the webbed flipper
of her ex-husband, struggling with his clothes,

after the flock billowed at the train windows,
clacking beaks until one thoughtful daughter
splashed the glass with a red plastic hammer
and they took off like the opposite of snow,

Leda watched the wild black skies of Dundee
as the honking swathes grew extra-terrestrial,
and felt her womb clench in its shell of muscle,

suspecting a backlash from the new economy,
unable to guess the motives of these creatures,
or what kind of thing she bore, into what future.

String Theory

after Paul Adrian

If you see the flightpath of a startled pigeon
outside the train and it seems so much faster
with you heading one way and it the other,
each accelerating in the opposite direction,

the bird a line with its particular vibration
in space/energy, instants of lung and feather,
first space then bird then emptiness thereafter,
a certain birdness in the rattle of electrons

and the gaps between its molecules and cells
hold nothing more solid than a continual chain
of becomings and unbecomings – in parallel

to your own particular vibrations on the train –
then only the wavelengths of thought and coo
and a pane of glass separate pigeon and you.

Between the Lines

No smoking anywhere in this station.
Transport police are located at platform 3.
Please retain your ticket for inspection.
This station is monitored by CCTV.

Passengers: keep behind the yellow line.
Shannon sucks dicks. Cyclists dismount.
Keep your luggage with you at all times.
Do not use lift once fire alarm sounds.

Attention. Danger: overhead live wires.
Bicycles must be removed by 18th July.
Deck is a cunt. Break glass in case of fire.

In emergency press here and await reply.
Keep clear. Fire escape. Keep left. Way out.
Shannon + Deck 4eva. Preston & South.

To Half-Inchling

There is a world where your cells multiplied
like the atoms in the heart of a star, exploding
into eyes and heartbeats; where I would sing
impatient Twinkle-Twinkles long after midnight,

the bottle in your face; where you were baptized
with a name more permanent than Half-Inchling,
or Nearly-Was, or Three-Monther, wee Not-Thing,
Clot-Angel, Sean Angus or Schrödinger's Child;

a world where you grew into your full potential,
debating your right to picket angry commuters,
lipsticking napkins with your name and number;

where you grew into more than a clump of cells
and grunts overheard outside the bathroom door,
where it would have been legitimate to mourn.

The Story of Grace

And then there was a night when the train stopped
by a field halfway between Leuchars and Dundee,
and the world was in snow as far as she could see,
the moon ridiculously big, and despite her laptop

at her seat, the boys, the shop, she took the window,
dropped to the rocky track where an ankle twisted,
and soaked her jeans clambering up from the ditch
until she was scrambling across the uneven snow

taking the path of the stoat or the doe in the dark
aware of her muscles again and the edges of air
in her lungs, up her back, plunging into nowhere,

trailing warm plumes of breath beneath the stars
until the train left her with only her own sounds,
alone on the earth, wondering what happens now.

Sweeney's Song

Last night I dreamt I had a second penis,
a nestling chick. I knew it was the baby's.
Though I knew it was going to leave us
and slowly get reabsorbed into my body,

there was a comfort to it. The night before
I did my weights in the blue light of the telly,
working my triceps and flight muscles sore
as you flickered between two foreign movies.

Tonight I've stuck my head outside the train
with Dundee's lights splattered on the river,
my hair plastered to my skull like feathers

and I am barking like a gander in the rain.
There is so much of the world I do not know,
but I am coming home. I'm coming home.

The Pigeon on the Rafters of the Station of the Metro

who should be dead & cobble-trod last winter
one leg a stump & half a face aboil in tumours
drops curious this new hour off the station rafters

who knows the kickers from the fodder-droppers
& loops one group of diners to one empty table over

now to tug a bagel from the bagel paper
incropped with grit & gum & bits of whopper

& a breeze down the gate ruffles up whose feathers

rainy salt air of the city rolling death-comes-quicker
poisoned corn & spikes stuck in dry corners
wide sky updarks the tumbling clouds of harbour

better live here where dust silts for watching over
better learn the patterned rabble dropping fodder

who fucked it once hops each new day thereafter

The Milk of My Craw

The craws of coastal birds are pockets of shell fragments
crusted with salt and grit and crinkled skin, as they crush
the dead members of the sea to a paste full of nutrients,

as the birds clamour over the spare limbs of a starfish,
warm frames of feathers carrying wet messages inside,
giving new life to the air by the sea's leftover flesh,

and I am aware of how sexual resentment can hide
as a poet tucks fears of castration within other images,
but am also aware that pigeons evolved on cliff-sides

and learned to home inland for seeds and potato wedges
and even the male pigeon's craw releases a thick matter
that will sustain the children while the mother forages

and I think my thoughts and watch our eldest daughter
chase flocks of geese to the tide, and I feed the infant
with chewed-up pieces of cracker and bottled water.

The Early Days

Some days the rainy glass so refracted the sunlight
that the sun shone like a bee's compound eye,

> as I fretted bills from desktop to teapot to bed
> with honey spread thick on the toasted heel of the bread,

as you walked back from the late shift at work,
bee-large raindrops pasting your skin to your shirt,

> and if I said gender was a choice in the pupal growth,
> steps in a dance flourishing in distinct roles,

you sang for a world where gender was meaningless,
the whole wet map spread flat below the both of us,

> and if I buzzed over an assemblage of facts
> to dissect details in my heart's thorax,

you saw lucidly, reflecting the world
with a light as transparent as it was cold,

> and if I got toxic treading bees on the carpet,
> unable to suck out the sting in half-lotus myself,

you tired of the sting of rain on your face
and your shirt's eternal dampness,

> but some afternoons the warm drum of rain
> faded to bees in the botanic gardens,

and you took pleasure in the slow hum
of pressure swelling inside the honeycomb,

                when I would see your skin and collapse
                    over you in a flush of raindrops,

that long April of daffodils blooming wildly,
of rain-spotted flowers rocking the odd sleeping bee,

            and sometimes we came upon the odd sleeping bee
              in rainy parks where daffodils bloomed wildly.

Like Animals

For Aisling and Kevin

On the worst days, when every breath is a pain,
I hope you find each other in the small hours,
lumbering on the cracked surfaces of your den,

and come back for the old moves, one arm here,
urgency dissolving heaviness from your torsos,
and the breath rises in your internal musculature

the way the silt rises in an abandoned dovecote
when it's windy outside and the dry air shakes
one long vowel, thrumming through the stones,

or the way manatees rise palely in shipwrecks,
clenching their palates on the long kelp blooms,
tugging the rigging until the tense stalks break

and after, stillness. All the badness will resume,
but I hope you encounter each other once again,
before sinking back in the darkness of the room.

The Rare Old Mountain Jig

after Jem Finer and Shane MacGowan

On Vigiljoch there's a room where our children dream of snow,
and moonlight whitens the dust on wind-chimes of goats' bones.

And if we rose for breath, we could blow in the goat's eyeholes,
and whistle up a rare old tune, a hey-diddle-di, diddle-day-die-o.

But some nights the only way to still the chorus of our stillborn
is slamming the breathless bodhráns of our bodies off each other.

And if we cannot face the music let us both face out the window,
in a jig of the twin-back beast, a hey-diddle-di, diddle-day-die-o.

Out there the glaciers ache for melting in the crags of Vigiljoch.
Pigeons huddle above the smokers in the eaves of the Bahnhoff.

In here a quickening reels us from the clenching of your womb,
as you spin to leave me kneeling in the far corner of the room.

Come hold the darkness from my chest. Don't let me die alone.
Soon the kids will wake and cry hey-diddle-di, diddle-day-die-o.

Nettles

Cabbage whites span in their giddy orbits.
Under her vest, nettles stroked her armpits,

softly sawing her a fresh coat of blisters.
I paused by her fallen bike, to watch her

pulse like phosphorus by the copper fence,
the way a silverback in Virunga's jungles

watches his young gnash mountain nettles
with wild pink tongues, stung by existence.

The Law of the Galapagos

*The project began in response to the massive ecosystem-wide destruction
caused by introduced goats on Alcedo Volcano on northern Isabela. At the
start [of] Project Isabela, the goat population on northern Isabela was
estimated at 100,000 animals.*

         – Galapagos Conservancy on Project Isabela

Grizzlehocks first flicks his lobes onto the rotor's noise
hind-legging for hung moss atop a saddle-neck tortoise

as the bullet yanks his left horn in splinters from his skull
and he belts, bleating like a kid, up the goat-cropped hill

and the helicopter tilts around at a forty-five-degree angle
to let the gunman reset his bead along his swinging rifle

and the goat yelps as three sharp pocks open up the dust
and leaps over the chewed remains of a mountain cactus,

and he is running out of land, his throat is hot and rare
as the after-bur that comes from chewing prickly pears,

until a shale of volcanic clinkers where his hoofing slips
and all Isabela spreads before him like the apocalypse,

with Judas-goats corralling recluse herds in makeshift runs
of piled carcasses warped and humming in the midday sun

as two giant tortoises rut tectonically on the rocks below,
beaks arching skywards from the foot of Volcan Alcedo,

and even as the hollow-point bites into Grizzlehocks' head,
in the moment before his jelled electrics go clinically dead

and his eyes invert to look upon everything that he has lost,
he still will not have understood the laws of the Galapagos.

The Pigeon on Electric Cables

we who dodged the death of passengers
tournaments & canneries & casseroles & laughter
& multiple solemn inquests held decades thereafter

yes we who made the century soaking rafters
now huddle charged on wires between steel towers

tho some of we who take off a touch clumsier
whose wingspan bridges wires to one another
rattle a spastic fire between the shoulders

carcassed upon tarmac lungs asmoulder

yes we who judge breadth careful as no other

see automobilised harries pass oblivious hereunder
squinting satnavs & ipads in general unbothered
only looking up if shadows take the weather

not mindful of the lost cumulus of passengers
or we who clutch electrics humming slaughter

bristling bilious static through whose feathers
veins drunk athrum on cables whispering power
whose guts count voltage by outliving massacres

who store offwing the mutterings of thunder

The Grey Gears of the Rain

i.

There were mornings my father sat on the edge of the bed
with one leg in his jeans, staring down into the other leg,
as if the hole could look back and see right into his brain

and understand. As if he was staring down a tunnel of rain
where he dimly made out the hunched forms of his future,
where fresh-faced soldiers trained rifles on his daughters,

as fathers glowered smoking in the grey corners of Derry,
and the rain churned and gyred its steel gears over the city,
and he would sit until one of us came in crying for lunch,

our eyes as blank as a greyhound's, at which he'd grunt
and thrust his foot in the other leg, suddenly embarrassed
at being caught alone again, in the half-light, at half-mast.

ii.

These days, every time I meet the grey whorl of his eyes,
I size him up for the heft I'll be shouldering when he dies,
heavier now than when he blacked out on the radiator pipe

that scalded skin off his neck, much heavier than as a child
when his lungs went black. His grey eyes churn multiverses,
a teenage kicking in a chippie after a dispute over manners,

or skidding off the Glenshane Pass into the back of a tractor,
soured clams and brandies bringing on the ruin of his liver,
events both cardiac and pulmonary, the systematic collapse

of his alimentary canal, fireworks bursting in his synapses,
even a universe where he holds the hand of my eldest child
while my own squat box swirls in the wet greys of his eyes.

Kraken Rising

The ink-sac bursts. I hold it up to let my daughter see,
flour the rings, fry them and plate up deep-fried squid.

That night she wakes screaming about the dead squid,
whether it hurts being dead, and if she really has to die.

I tell her great nets of squid will wash onboard and die,
so fishermen bring money home at the end of the night.

I lift her to the window to see the wide Sardinian night
naming the Big Dipper, the North Star and Andromeda.

I tell her life is massive; how Perseus saved Andromeda
unchaining her just in time to hang her name on a galaxy.

I tell of supernovas and light and that even a dead galaxy
is bright for centuries; how we swim the cells and dreams

of kids and lovers when we die. But she's back in dreams,
and I feel like Cepheus as he turned from the bubbling sea.

The Frog Prince

There is nothing that can be done in this green world
about a boy with the stench of pond-water in his burps

creaking to your daughter's en-suite while she sleeps,
where he stumbles upon a leak in his jellied sheath

and his eyes bulge like spawn dilating in the mirror,
envisioning a foam of his own generational matter

stewing inside her as tadpoles stew in shallow water,
and the world darkens as he struggles to remember

a story about a pond so green it was almost brown,
and how the fern-tips rattled as a frog pushed down

past their pale roots, reaching the pond's rank bottom
where a golden ball blazed a nova in the pond-scum

and it thunders outside, and a sudden thump of green
webs the skylight in fractures, reddening at the seams,

as beyond the curtains the suburbs bathe in a holy rain,
frogs splattering on jeeps and birdbaths in bony stains

as the middle classes stare across their bloodied patios,
and you skid off the tarmac, trapped inside your Volvo

and on the bonnet, a lone frog is bellowing, unharmed
in a world cart-wheeling with wild dogs and car alarms

and your daughter raises her head to ask what is amiss
and the boy croaks, halfway between a ribbet and a kiss.

The Beast of the Galapagos

after Kurt Vonnegut

I bear her over the mad waves,
her armbands left on the sand.
She squeals like an otter pup,
and I miss the breaker behind,

her armbands left on the sand,
as she crashes from my reach,
and I miss the breaker behind,
my throat fills with the ocean,

as she crashes from my reach,
like wreckage, Europe, meteors,
my throat fills with the ocean,
awash with viruses and floods,

like wreckage, Europe, meteors,
through the genealogical chain
awash with viruses and floods,
and the only humans to surface

through the genealogical chain
gnash crabs with blunt molars,
and the only humans to surface,
oval eyes rolling in flat skulls,

gnash crabs with blunt molars,
rising groggily from the depths,
oval eyes rolling in flat skulls,
and my fingers stroke her skull

rising groggily from the depths,
twisted blind in breathlessness,
and my fingers stroke her skull,
and I bruise her against my ribs,

twisted blind in breathlessness.
She squeals like an otter pup,
and I bruise her against my ribs.
I bear her over the mad waves.

The Sins of the Otter

Eleven chicken strangled and she only took the eggs.
Gnawed the heads off Sally's koi and tossed the rest,
never mind the dog's dinner or the emptied riverbeds.

Swans paraded a fresh viciousness around their nests.
Dave taught me how to trace her scat back to the holt
and I nearly had her, shoulder-deep, holding my nose

from the soured fug of piss and fish around the hole,
but all I got was a handful of air. The bitch had bolted.
Dave got her in the end though. He said the worst thing

wasn't her yipping, the hump of her or the grassy stink,
but her fury for the river when he swung the trap open,
and on the long drive home, his cage's hollow rattling.

The Pigeon on Rubble

we whose lungs cool once burnt tyres settle
when dust hides from the wind in orange puddles

who ledge in split brickwork by the hospital
who belly hatchlings & watch on high for eagles
when trucks make space inland for new arrivals

we who pluck fresh nests from cracked enamel
burnt suitcases & tupperware & adidas in shrapnel

bend in new tunnels to bodies in the rubble
dead eye to eye converse with harry's people
claim their softer grubs to carry up whose steeples

o love is many winged & outlasts engine throttles

& we who breed in brief humps on the windowsills
live kiss by kiss to balance love with what is edible
plump we who oversit each city like a dining table

The Dance of Ararat

after W C Williams

If my wife is snoring as softly as a musk-ox,
the child purring in the cot, and a distant hum
declares the taxis and rain have nearly stopped,

and my empties are strewn like a planetarium
in the aquatic light of my screensaver, as I rise
and feel the deck shift under the living room

but catch myself in an arabesque, and the line
of muscle in my forearm seems a thing of glory,
and behold, my hard calves, buttocks and thighs

and sense the thousands in the darkness, more,
a disco of silent limbs around me and each one
heaving their breaths, ecstatic, owning the floor,

then who is to say I am less than Noah, captain
waiting for the tide to breach against the top
of Ararat, one hand steady on the klaxon?

On the Fifth Day

A man as portly as a god was undoing every latch
on the shelves in his van, releasing all his pigeons
over a crook in the coast, and I had to stop jogging.

Inside the buggy, I heard the child's breath catch
as they pulsed their white bellies across creation,
the world filling with wings and the sound of wings.

Acknowledgements

Some of these poems or versions of them appeared in the following magazines: *The London Magazine; The Frogmore Papers; Poetry Ireland Review; Poetry London; Poetry Wales; Poetry Proper; The Virginia Quarterly Review; The Chatahoochee Review; Tears in the Fence; Magma.*

Some poems here have been shortlisted or highly commended in the Manchester Poetry Prize, the Bridport Prize and the Wigtown International Poetry Prize, and have appeared in the publicity materials for the respective prize's associated events.

A number of these poems have been recorded for *The Writing Life* and for www.fishhousepoems.org.

Thanks are due to Amy Wack, and all editors and parties involved. Particular thanks are due to Jacob Riglin for the cover photo, and Paul Maddern for the author photo.

To the friends who read and shared advice on my poems over the years, thank you.

Most of all, thanks to Katja, Roisín and Leonie. You guys rock.

Also by Eoghan Walls

The Salt Harvest

'What separates The Salt Harvest *from many first collections is a willingness to look for the poetic in pretty much anything, an almost aureate diction, and a darkly exuberant style. The vigour and reach of* The Salt Harvest *makes Walls a poet worth watching.'*
— The Guardian

'Walls wields a voice which strikes out on its own and, like all the best poetic voices, seems almost entirely to lack antecedents … here, "praise be", is a voice bringing something really new.'
— The Edinburgh Review

'One distinctive feature of The Salt Harvest *is the really accomplished exploitation of rhyme and various forms of pararhyme, refrain and repetition. Equally notable is Walls's deft harnessing of traditional poetic forms, among them terza rima, the ghazal and the villanelle. He is also alert to the possibilities of phrasing: 'Osiris and the Prague Flood', a poem of forty lines, is a single sentence strung out almost in the manner of Emily Dickinson with a series of dashes. At the other end of the spectrum, 'Tourists at S.21' dares to consider a notorious Khmer Rouge prison and its victims within the confines of six lines. These poems certainly merit re-reading and will reward the reader's perseverance.'*
— The Warwick Review

'There is a tangy, tactile sensibility to Eoghan Walls' strange harvest — from the shifting demographic of today's Europe to the ancient Olympians and their contemporary galactic namesakes, from deserted air-terminals to obscure taxonomies, from a lone boiled egg to the stoical and grim crop reaped by migrant workers. Wall's bold poetic hovers fruitfully between taste and sense, between intellect and lore, between the continuity of family and the fragmentations of history, between the matter and musculature of humanity:* The Salt Harvest *is a collection that, in its shimmering linguistics and steadfast gaze, will speak directly to our fraught and familiar world.'*
— Anne-Marie Fyfe

'The old world is finished, The Salt Harvest *tells us, and I am terrified. From Derry to Drogheda to eastern Europe and Beyond, an aluminium angel with a frogsoul contemplates the meat and animals of a dry world darkening, probes starmatter in vain for limbo, titillates with leftover words like pray or sacrament in a negative baptism where nithing is as funny as it used to be. A griefdappled dirgebook lifted alive by love from the water.'*
— Medbh McGuckian

SEREN
Well chosen words

Seren is an independent publisher with a wide-ranging list which includes poetry, fiction, biography, art, translation, criticism and history. Many of our books and authors have been on longlists and shortlists for – or won – major literary prizes, among them the Costa Award, the Jerwood Fiction Uncovered Prize, the Man Booker, the Desmond Elliott Prize, The Writers' Guild Award, Forward Prize and TS Eliot Prize.

At the heart of our list is a beautiful poem, a good story told well or an idea or history presented interestingly or provocatively. We're international in authorship and readership though our roots are here in Wales (Seren means Star in Welsh), where we prove that writers from a small country with an intricate culture have a worldwide relevance.

Our aim is to publish work of the highest literary and artistic merit that also succeeds commercially in a competitive, fast changing environment. You can help us achieve this goal by reading more of our books – available from all good bookshops and increasingly as e-books. You can also buy them at 20% discount from our website, and get monthly updates about forthcoming titles, readings, launches and other news about Seren and the authors we publish.

www.serenbooks.com